YOUR KNOWLEDGE HAS VALUE

Womanhood in Tiv Literary Genres. A Reinterpretation of Gender Roles in an African Society

Alloy S. Ihuah

Bibliographic information published by the German National Library:

The German National Library lists this publication in the National Bibliography; detailed bibliographic data are available on the Internet at http://dnb.dnb.de.

ISBN: 9783346584649
This book is also available as an ebook.

© GRIN Publishing GmbH
Nymphenburger Straße 86
80636 München

Print and binding: Books on Demand GmbH, Norderstedt, Germany
Printed on acid-free paper from responsible sources.

The present work has been carefully prepared. Nevertheless, authors and publishers do not incur liability for the correctness of information, notes, links and advice as well as any printing errors.

GRIN web shop: https://www.grin.com/document/1163000

WOMANHOOD IN TIV LITERARY GENRES: REINTERPRETING GENDER ROLES IN AN AFRICAN SOCIETY

Alloy, S. Ihuah, PhhD

Abstract

The Tiv of Middle-Belt Nigeria are a unique ethnic nationality whose feminine gender is regarded as the heart-beat of the house holder, the measure of all things for the husband and the epicenter of the community. Contrary to the conclusion of the African Neo-cultural positivists, the roles Tiv traditional social system assigns to the feminine gender noble roles that elevate than demean her status as a womwn. She is neither marginalized nor oppressed and exploited in social, political, economic and religious spheres. Gender discrimination is *sine qua non* in traditional society though, it is benevolent. The paper argues further that, redemption from discrimination for the kwase Tiv is neither found in liberating her, for she is not enslaved, nor in centering her, she is the epicenter of the house holder. Womanhood in her feminine roles supplements and compliments the men for universal beneficence; the common good of Tiv society. She has womb, kitchen and cradle, but in further empowerment of her female power. We conclude that the roles tradition assigns to women are meant to advance the anatomy of their female power to receive life's impulses to husband its stability and persistence of Tiv society. Woman is a female, and man is a male, different as biological facts though, they both seek in each, the other and the being of their beings.

Key Words: Womanhood, Tiv Woman, Kwase Tiv, Gender Discrimination, Empowerment, Gender Centering

1

Table of Contents

Introduction... 3

Feminism and Tiv Society 4

Gender in Tiv Literary Genres.. 12

The Positive Tiv Woman 16

Conclusion 20

REFERENCES 22

Introduction

To be a woman you really are, to perform your vital role for your family and society as a woman, and to reap the rich rewards of love and fulfillment that are yours as a women, you must refuse to reject your fundamental nature as a woman-Mrs. Monica, A. Ushir-Hou.[1]

The 20th century has witnessed a powerful wave throughout the world to spiritually and socially uplift women and liberate them from the domination of men. This agitation was carried on through the Beijing Conference of 1995 with the popular belief that human progress as a whole depends on the spiritual, social, psychological and economic empowerment of women who are, without any good reason, discriminated against. Acolytes of this theory posit in no unmistaken language that, women world-wide suffer discrimination and oppression, and so they are in need of both liberation, centering and empowerment. The question of whether this thinking finds placement in every other African ethnic community is of concern to us in this paper. This work argues that, among the Tiv of central Nigeria *kwase ka ishima I orya* i.e. the wife is the epicenter of the house holder, the measure of all things for the husband and the epicenter of the community.

Contrary to the conclusion of the African Neo-cultural positives, the roles Tiv traditional social system assigns to *kwase Tiv* do not demean her and makes her interior. She is neither marginalized nor oppressed and exploited in social, political, economic and religious spheres. We argue that though gender discrimination is sine qua non in traditional Tiv social system, it is benevolent. That :redemption" from discrimination for the *kwase Tiv* is neither found in liberating her, for she is not enslaved, nor in centering her, she is the epicenter of the house holder, she has womb, kitchen and cradle, but in further empowerment of her female power. We conclude that the roles tradition assigns to women are meant to advance the anatomy of the female power to receive life's impulses to husband its stability and persistence of Tiv society. *Kwase* Tiv, it is contended here, needs further empowerment, not liberation and centering or equality. By the instrumentality of traditional

---

[1] This was the candid view of **Mrs. Monica, Ushir** *a house wife of over thirty years' experience. Her views in this regard is golden*

3

Tiv governance system, Kwase Tiv is a creature whose being attain true essential human nature through complementarity and suplementarity.

Feminism and Tiv Society

Tiv social operates a dual-sex system in which men and women have distinctive roles. This explains their variegated cultural attitudes subsumed in a sexist ideology. In itself, sexism is the principle of using the differences between male and female human beings as a criterion for determining the social worth and rights of men and women in society. Three levels of sexism are here addressed. Benevolent sexism preaches sympathy with women along side children as weaker vessels who need support and empowerment. Tiv social system practices this in excess as the local expression has it *kwase hemen ityav ga;* woman, the life giver does not risk life in wars. In the west, one of the more dynamic examples of benevolent sexism concerned the issue of who had priority to use the life boats while the Titanic was sinking in April 1912. Women and children, it was decided would have priority of access to the life boats[2]. Benign sexism recognizes gender segregation without bestowing sexual advantage or inflicting a gender cost. It is harmless sexism which finds expression among the Tiv in names and ritual ceremonies which celebrate womanhood. Tiv names like *Torkwase* (Queen Mother) *Hembadoon* (Female is the best child) *Iember* (Bundle of joy) are few examples in point. It is also not out of point to state that the wide spread practice of polygamy, and the payment of bride-price are benign sexism (or benign polygamy) in expression. The women who as it were, are more in number than the men are brought together from varied backgrounds and made to establish a dialogic encounter, to create a community with the husband as the head. On the second count, women in Tiv society are treasured as supreme realities, essential beings, and the over-yonder towards which life tends; the Mother, the wife on whom anything and everything is invaluable. The third category, malignant or malevolent sexism is the most pervasive and most insidious gender ideology. It views every woman as inferior to every man and concludes there from that both cannot have equal rights. In most societies, it subjects women to economic manipulation, sexual exploitation and political

---

[2] For a detailed story, read Mazrui, A.A. (1991) "The Black Woman and the Problem of Gender. Trials Triumphs and Challenges" Being the 1991 Guardian Lecture Delivered on July 4, 1991.

marginalization. Tiv society recognizes this ideology though, its practice is limited to women of transgressed character known among the Tiv as *Kasev-Mba-hemban-ato;* the negative Tiv women.

While there are some ethnographic data on the basis of which a case can be made for the assignment of interior roles and status to women in traditional Tiv society, such ethnographic data are however defective and unhelpful on two counts. On the first count, the data fail to go the whole way in viewing the status and role of women as part of a complex totality of Tiv customs and social values.

Taking into account the unique nature of the Tiv outlook on the created world, its comprehensiveness, its communality, and its egalitarian, rural and agrarian nature, traditional Tiv social system consigns to women the roles and status that best agree with the common will, social control and group goals and objectives. The role and status of a sister *(ingnor),* a housewife *(Kwase yough),* a mother (Ngo) and divorce *(wan ya)* are different one from the other. In any or some of these roles, her position may be viewed as "interior" and an "underprivileged". Yet, in any or some of these roles, her position may be viewed as "superior" and privileged". In Tiv understanding however, the woman's role and status is more or less at par with that of the man. This position is well illustrated by Angya (1999) who argues that in any conjugal association, the husband plays the leading role. "The Tiv", she says "do not give to the courage of women the same form or the same direction as to that of men, but they never doubt her courage; and if they hold that man and his partner ought to not always exercise their intellect to be as that of other too"[3]. Angya argues further like Simone de Beauvior that, the division between the sexes is not the product of an event in history, instead, this division "is a biological fact". Women are women; she says; by virtue of their anatomy and physiology, and throughout history, they have always been subordinated to men[4]. Even though this thinking is embellished with the alloys of the modern Tiv women, one salient fact which reflects the spirit of the past is its egalitarian fair.

The Tiv do not think that man and woman have either the duty or the right to perform the same roles, but they show an equal regard for both their respective part; and though their lot is

---

[3] Charity Angya, (Professor and Director, Centre for Gender Studies/Experienced House wife. Recorded interview in Makurdi on 20 August,2002 at Makurdi.
[4] Beauvoir, S. (1993) The Second Sex in Stumpf, S.E, Elements of Philosophy: An Introduction New York, McGrow-Hill, Inc.p160

different, they consider both of them as beings of equal value though, like any successful vehicles must have only one person on the wheel with ultimate responsibility. Most obviously, Saint Paul's words in Ephesians 5:22-28 apply succinctly to the Tiv. "Wives, submit yourselves unto your own husbands ... for the husband is the head..."

Evidently, clear traits of malevolent discriminatory practices are absent in traditional Tiv social relations. Tiv oral texts abundantly support the thesis that the opportunities of the Tiv woman to achieve her desires are no less than man's, what defines social relationship include among others metaphysical prowess, power and authority, wealth and the age question. They define the individual's behaviour in terms of who behaves where, and in the presence of who. Thus the Tiv talk of *Or Kwav* (age mate) with whom one is an equal in social interaction. Those who are *Kwav* share between one to two years gap. Kopytoff more lucidly expresses this idea thus: "Lineage authority and representation of the lineage to the outside world are organized on continuum of age that is of relative eldership... Thus, the inequality of power and authority is most pronounced between generations and it is thus presumptuous for the junior generation to question the decision of the senior generation"[5].

Professor C.S Momoh's (1978:41) generalization most aptly sums up the thinking of the Tiv. According to him, the way African (Tiv) traditional thought had structured things in society was such that old age came first. On this basis authority, discipline and respect was to flow. It so happens that in traditional marriages, the husband was often the older and so automatically, by the cannons of the social custom he assumes leadership in the partnerships[6].

In Tiv marriages, this cultural trait merges as an invaluable index of social relationship. Thus, the wife obeys and respects her husband not only because he is the head of the family but also because he is elder and the husband controls and directs the wife because she is younger.

Yam-she by which definition is giving out ones' sister *ingor* in exchange for another persons' sister is said to devalue womanhood though, as a wife". It was rather a potent means of preserving the basic cultural value of the Tiv by retaining the reproductive force within the

---

[5] Kopytorff T, I. "Ancestors as Elders," in Africa Vol. 41 No. 2. 1971 p128
[6] Momoh, C.S.(1978) "Eldership in African Marriages" in African Insight, Vol. 18 No. 1. Spring. P41

community, far from the half truths or outright fabrication that are intent at constructing a blind maze around the true essential being of *Kwase Tiv,*

What is said to be the demeaning status of women today is the result of the abolition of the traditional marriage system. *Yam-she* was a powerful deterrent against tribal disintegration. With its abolition, tradition and custom, and the authority of the elders were easily repudiated. So *tar Tiv vihi* (Tivland was distressed). The bride-price *(Kem-kwase).* Thus, it became obvious that wives secured under this new system were not tied to any control measure, and so the women (wives) could leave their husbands with the flimsiest excuse. Perhaps this is what accounts for the present day demeaning roles and discriminatory practices against women. The Dutch Reformed Christian Missionary **(DRCM),** Casalegio agrees with this conclusion; *this bride-price marriage which was looked forward to with such great expectation degenerated from its inception into commerce in human lives[7].*

True, the abolition of Yam-she enhanced the position of women because they now had a greater choice of marriage partners or at least a voice in the selection, it also reduced immorality in Tiv community by enabling the young to marry with personal funds as at when due. But it also hastened the atomization of the Tiv community, and demeaned motherhood in the process. In Tiv social system in which exchange marriage subsisted, the fertility of the wife was enhanced by *akombo* a spiritual force which was placed outside the house of the wife. The sons that came from this marriage "set right" this akombo when necessary to secure health and fertility for their own wives.

Clearly, womanhood was central to Tiv ontology and apparently, motherhood, as espoused above, represented the principle of the fecundity of the family, even though she was a woman of another compound. The shattering of this social system and the emergence of kem-kwase eroded the esteemed status of womanhood and invariably disintegrated the community spirit which its essence, the Tiv cherished and guarded jealously. As a consequence, says Rubingh,

> *"the tribe now stood in danger of supernatural affliction, for the means to protect against human pollution had been removed. There was no adequate way to guard*

---

[7] Rubingh, E. (1969) Sons of Tiv, Grande Rapids, Michigan, Baker Book House Company.`p134

miscarriage, abundant conception… now the possessors of evil tsav (witchcraft) could move in to strike at their defenseless victims at will"[8]

Thus far, womanhood in Tiv social system is holism. She is related to nature to form wholes that are more than the sum of the parts b y creative evolution. She is related to the earth and embodied the same fertility as the earth; the natural repercussions in the yield of the fields could be ominously foretold. Such is the status of Tiv women as mothers that the Tiv find a way acknowledging same in names by directly replicating the name of their dead grandmothers or sisters.

In Tiv society, entire community has a stake in the marriageable females *(angor).* So argues Rubingh (1969:135) "if there were many daughters born rather than sons, this was no real loss, for they could be exchanged for additional wives"[9] either for himself, his sons and, or distressed members of the immediate community who work on his farm. Thus, through *angor,* creativity, and hence continuity of animate and inanimate beings is sustained. The Tiv, therefore, celebrate the arrival of female children as many as they came. This celebration finds expression in names and ritual ceremonies. It is thus common to find such praise names as Hembadoon (the best); lember (my bundle of joy) Doobee (perfect finish); Afazende (one with a majestic walk); Kumashe (the esteemed woman); Dookwase (the beautiful one); Torkwase (Queen mother), which all point to the fact that womanhood in traditional Tiv society is the over-wonder toward which life tends.

The next question concerns the status of a woman as a divorcee or an unmarried member of the society (i.e. *Wan Yd}.* This category of women has been reclassified into two units. Firstly, those who suffered primary bareness and are tired of 'working for other people's children.". The second group include those who may have been divorced by their husbands for whatever reason or those whose bride price may not have been paid, Whichever category they belong, traditional Tiv social system recognized them as full-blooded members of the society who in truth are the connecting rod, of continuity between men, the cosmos and nature.

The observation of Ruth Laudes (1953:126) correctly applies to the Tiv, that "throughout Africa, women traditionally have been accorded extensive opportunities... and official recognition (as Priestesses, and mediums... and other authorities supervising women's interest"[10] in politics

---

[8] *ibid*
[9] Ibid p135
[10] Ruth Laudes in Rubingh, E. (1969) Sons of Tiv, Grande Rapids, Michigan, Baker Book House Company.p126

and economy. The case of official recognition of women's status and role in traditional Tiv society explains the election in 1999 of a widow, Mrs. Margaret Icheen, the first female speaker of a house of Assembly in Africa (i.e. in the Benue State House of Assembly). This is in addition to the very many women traditional title holders found all over Tivland.

Division of labour is another parameter for measuring the status of women in traditional societies. The division of labour between husband and wife either with respect to the upbringing of children or to the production of food for consumption; that between girls and boys as regards the functions expected of them by their family and the community at large and that between men and women as members of the community. This delineation fits the Tiv social system very well. There are roles that are strictly feminine while others are Male defined. The differential roles are consigned by the divine architect in acknowledgment of the physiology of the sexes. Sigmud Freud provides for us a typical example when he says that the moral sensibility of women differs from those of men. Quoting Freud, S.E. Stumpf (1993:114) says;

> *cannot evade the notion (though I hesitate to give it expression) that for women the level of what is ethically normal is different from what it is in men. Their superego is never inexorable, so impersonal, so independent for its emotional origins as we require it to be in men. Character - traits which critics of every epoch have broughtup against women - that they show less sense of justice than men, that they are less ready to submit to the great exigencies of life, that they are more often influenced in their judgements by feelings of affection or hostility - all these -would be aptly accounted for by the modification in the formation of their superego[11].*

Piaget is more outward in his observations about the nature of morality in women as compared to the men. In this study of the rules of children's games, he observed that, in the games they played, girls were "less explicit about agreement (than boys) and less concerned with legal elaboration". In contrast to the boy's interest in the codification of rules, the girls adopted a more pragmatic attitude, regarding "a rule as good so long as the game brings reward. Thus, in comparison to the boys, the girls were found to be "more tolerant and more easily reconciled to innovation"[12]

---

[11] Stumpf, S.E. (1993) Elements of Philosophy; An Introduction (3rd Edition) McGraw-Hill Book Company/
[12] Amao - Kehinde, A,O. (2000) A Course text on human Development and Learning, Lagos.p126

Farming in Tiv society is a hared role. But the man prepares the land and tills the land, while the woman weeds the farm, harvests and gathers the proceeds for storage. By calculation, the Tiv woman perform sixty to seventy percent of this role (farming) which she understand and interprets as the functional role of a housewife as the chief welfare officer of the family. Understandably, her role in agriculture, though more than that of the man, is not construed as a form of injustice, oppression and or suppression, or even exploitation. The man takes up other socio-traditional roles of *tar-sorun* (governance through *akombo* ritual, *Mba-mzough* (meetings) and *Ijir I orun* (Moot or judicial functions) between aggrieved parties to engender an all round family development. It suffices to say then that Kwase Tiv wielded reasonable political authority, economic power and social influence in the pre-colonial period than at any time in Nigeria.

Perhaps this point is more ably captured by Chinweizu, (Ityavyar, 1992:12-13) that women Ipso facto have political power. Women, he say, have more political power than men, because women have the womb, kitchen and cradle. As he put it;

> *Everyday of man's life, he is subject to the dictates of womb, kitchen and cradle. The first set to rule him belongs to his mother; the second belongs to his wife. The first rules him in his invulnerable infancy. The second in his ambitious adulthood. His bride exploits his nostalgia for his mother's set and manipulates his craving for his future wife. This mother, bride and wife control a man everyday of his life by playing on his changing needs for womb, kitchen and cradle. The power of the womb is great. It holds the mightiest of men.*[13]

This thinking is suggestive of the invisible hand of the women in determining men's actions. It suggests that "men rule the world but women rule men", that men are leaders, but they are led by women. Tiv society reflects the same social behaviour. A Tiv praise singer captures this allusion cryptically thus:

> *Mbatsev Kpa Yange Kwase agba ve sha Shima kpishi ve vaa nan. Aginde Genaju Yange nee amo kpa vaan Mbasue. Kuje Yum ngu vaan Dondoaor. Yange Abuul Benga Ncfyer hemba Mbagwa Pulututu kpa wan-Menda tema. Sha ukuna shala Tor Achir Ikima Toga Yange nee Tor cii. Una or Kwagh asor Wan-Jobella...*

---

[13] Ityavyar, D. (1992) The Changing socio-political role of Tiv women, Jos, University of Jos Press.

*(our forebears also mourned the woman -who their hearts trust in her **Aginde Genaju**, the most famous praise singer mourned his wife **Mbasue, Kuje Yum** is mourning **Dondoaor, chief Abuul Benga Ndyer**, ruled the entire **Mbagwa** clem draconially, though his wife **Wan-Menda** ruled him. **Chief Acchir Ikima Taga**, an acclaimed maximum ruler of Kunav clam, swore by the name of **WanOJabela**, his wife before making any policy decision).*

Understandably, there is a whole world of significance which exists only through woman, she is the substance of men's acts and sentiments, the incarnation of all the values that call out their free activity. For the Tiv, therefore, woman is all that man desires, a god mediatrix between propitious nature and man. the picture presented above clearly illuminates the esteemed and central position of the Tiv women in contrast to the imaginary women of the functionalists. Indeed, the Tiv of the Middle Belt are one among the very few African ethnic groups wherein women occupy important social, political and religious positions in the society. In Tiv metaphysical thought, man and woman are equipremodially disclosed in the world, hence, a successful society depends on a delicate balancing of different (male and female) factors.

Tiv women also have a big role in the economy. Their labour is in no way exploited by their husbands., this truism is pointed out with great clarity by P. and L Bohannan that,

When a Tiv woman gives her husband Yam's, the amount is never stipulated and she may well argue. In no case does she give enough to enrich her husband a portion of that money. She spends the money for food, clothing for herself or her children, soap and perfume. Men do not, indeed cannot exploit the labour or the produce of their women. Women from the nearby Udam tribes say they like to marry Tiv men because they treat their wives well[14].

All these are cases of female empowerment in Tiv society. It thus argues that, sustainability of Tiv civilization is founded on solidarity of the family. It is based on man and woman, together, enacting complimentary roles.

---

[14] P. and L Bohannan

11

Gender in Tiv Literary Genres

Kwase do jo; Kwase ka ikondo I-njaa, Kase ne or hembe shagba, Shi kwase ka ana or nanzuaaku... {OliverAye
Wife is treasure. It is a valued apparel. It begets honour and prestige though, it is a source of death).

Phyllis Schlafly records the reply of one of the most successful writers of the twentieth century, Taylor Cladwell, who was asked by *Family Weekly,* an American Magazine if it did not give her solid satisfaction to know that her novel, Captains and the Kings was to be watched as a nine-hour television production. Her reply.

There is no solid satisfaction in any career for a woman like myself. There is no hope, no true freedom, no home, no joy, no expectation for tomorrow, no contentment. I would rather cook a mealfor a man and bring him his slippers and feel myself in the protection of his arms than have all the citations and awards and honours. I have received worldwide, including the Ribbon of the Legion of Honour and my property and my bank accounts.[15]

Talking with Tiv women and ransacking the entire corpus of Tiv oral texts confirms that such conclusion is in perfect agreement with the thinking of the positive Tiv women. The above conclusion is only one chapter of womanhood in traditional Tiv social thought. There are found also in Tiv society a tiny tribe of negative women *(Kasev mba saan ishe).* Marriage and motherhood, they argue, force women into subservient roles from which they must be liberated. Satisfaction and joy for them in our contemporary world is outside the walls of man's house. Their thinking is that there is greater career satisfaction in being elected to important positions, traveling to exciting faraway places, having executive authority over large numbers of people and earning a financial fortune. These women shout at and command men and women that, me *yameu kua tsombur wou* i.e. I will buy you and your entire lineage.

Thus, marriage and womanhood which give a woman a new identity and opportunity for an all round fulfillment is construed by this category of women as servitude and intolerable. But who is a housewife? The Oxford English Dictionary defines housewife as "a woman (usually a married woman) who manages or directs the affairs of her household: the mistress of the family:

---

[15] *(Schlafty, 1978:20).*

the wife of the householder; often, a woman who manages her household with skills and thrift, a domestic economist".[16] The Tiv give her a more professional management status as a home executive: planning, organizing, leading, co-ordinating and controlling. She can set her own schedule and standards and have her freedom of choice to engage in everything from children to civic work, politics to gardening. She is thus understood as the representative of the principles of the fecundity of the family, and as one who has complete control of the food supply and authority in domestic affairs. Such is the woman who is respected, honoured and esteemed. As a housewife, she is the husband's incarnate. Indeed, she knows the secretes of her husband and those concerning the affairs of the clan.

On the one handy is the positive Tiv woman who is quick to identify the pillars of a happy marriage and so combines appreciation and admiration with cheerfulness to magnet her man to the walls of a family house. She has stolen her husband's heart; *$ ishima I orya* and is a perfect good likened to a special cloth, a treasure which brings prestige and honour to the husband. Such a woman is code named *Pendatyo* i.e the husband's headrest. She is willing to give her husband the appreciation and the admiration which his manhood craves. She is extremely strong willed to temperament and independent in act. She speaks with authority and is forceful to the point of being domineering in her dealing with her fellow human beings; female and male. But for her husband, the relationship is that of the dutiful wife, deferring always to her husband's wishes in her domestic partnership. She makes the husband believe that, to him alone is all the world. She is submissive and more abnegating than any wife in the environ. She often seats beside her husband with the right hand across the husband shoulders, i.e *har nom na ityaugh sha kwende* to share life's joys and sorrows.

The Tiv describe them as *gbenger er ka iho* i.e. knife without a handle. Society A does not assign to them esteemed roles, *kasev mba i goom ve ibor udam.* They are abandoned as society wives, as mere labourers, Kureve (2002) is apt in his description of this category n that, *shima I bume kwase ngi shin tyo.* i.e. (the mind-set of the negative woman is in her sexy looks). Like a floppy diskette, Kuleve vouches further that, the woman's entire life secrets are laid bare once the password is decoded through sexual intercourse. She is quick to divulge the entire secret life of

---

[16] The Oxford English Dictionary 1979:281

her husband to her lover and or family enemies. The heart of the husband does not trust her, Tiv tradition and custom acknowledge this thinking in Proverbs as follows;

Kwase ka amee aya (woman is a trickster)
kwase ka akpakunt ftmon) iabo uzeren kpa I agher. % (woman is akpakuru cloth, it is fitting though, it itches)
kwase ka ikya^, ka I a tsue I pose ahu
(woman is baboon. It is driven by self-interest/profit motive)
kyvase ke suswam, ka une bende awe awambe adue
(wman is hedges with whom every contact incurs its wrath.) A
kwffse ka kwagh u yon dor amin ga.,
(wman is not a being with whom oifgambles.).

As a house wife, the negative Tiv woman suffers from a dozen fallacies of mistaken notions that traditonal marriage is based on the wife's submerging her identity, in her husband's catering to his every whim, binding herself seven days and nights a week inside the four walls of the home, stultifying her intellectual or professional or community interests, and otherwise reducing herself to the caricature of a dumb helpless *oryese* i.e. home assistant,

Further and perhaps better understanding of the negative woman is incased in the following Tiv.

> Godwin Abuul (2002).
"kwase u a soo nom senden kwagh a nom u nan he tembe . Kpa kwase u a soo nom ga yo, nom ngu a penda a loo, Pue sule ka iyange mom tseghel. Kwase soo nom ngu a tachia er m ngu yan ichan kpa ka chi u mbayev av, kpa Kwase u soo nom ga yo ngue akaa er Imarem a wan ga, Kwagh wough la gande me yem Iwa iyam tar ga" .

(The woman who does not love her husband quarrels and misbehaves. When the husband says one thing, she replies him back in two folds. The woman who does not love her husband says children are "parasites" who must not encroach on her independent self. 1 am tired of you, I will go back to my father's house[17]).

> Nyam Ayua (2002) is even more revealing;
Kasev ka mhoonum ma Anyam, Ufa nan ga U yem tyough tingir.

Ka 1 gba pe u ver zwa pe nan lu kuan la,

(women is a poisonous substance, it takes knowledge and wisdom to taste; else yowill die. you have to know the direction of her thought to create a functional relationship).[18]

> *Anonymous*

---

[17] Abuul, G. (2000) Recorded interview in Makurdi on *fatf** May.
[18] Ayua, N. (2002) Praise Singer Cited Courtesy of Gwaza uja-Matyo, Broadcaster in Makurdi, recorded interview on 20th May.

\wti *Kasev mba I nja er ka we a* AP#T *wea na 1 luam sha nyam je kpa I mough iyem yon akongo . . .(women are like dogs, pet fed in the house with meat though, they still go out in search of excrements).*

The three songs reveal the true nature of the negative Tiv women, whose satisfaction and self fulfillment is outside the boundaries of conjugal association. In the first song, the most cherished ingredients of marriage and motherhood viz appreciation, admiration and cheerfulness are jettisoned. Children who are the most fulfilling dream of every woman are here said to be an obstacle in the face of other more fulfilling careers, The Tiv would say, she is *Bume kwase.* A woman of misguided mission and vision of life.

The second song portrays women as a killer substance. In the most captivating manner, the song paints a picture of an unpredictable being with the capacity to heal and kill, a paradox of a kind. The last song is more forceful. Women in its tone is anathema, who in body and soul is manifestly evil. In a tone which sounds biblical, woman is said to still groan in the dark even though light has come to the world, living in the world, full of "milk and honey" though, feeds on "vinegar", social relation with this category of women is akin to *uteen kpev shagondo we* i.e. tricks and dishonesty.

It is perhaps this image of womanhood that might have informed the experience of Kerkegaard in *States on the road to life,* "to be a woman ", he says "is something so strange, so confused, so complicated, that no one predicate comes near expressing it and that the multiple predicates that one would like to use are so contradictory that only a woman can put up with it"[19] (Stumpf, 1993:33), It suffices to say then that it is not nature that defines woman so negatively in the words above; it is woman who defines herself, by dealing with nature on her own account in her emotional life,

The Tiv are wont to argue however that such understanding is the gateway to the understanding of another chapter of womanhood; the positive woman through whom humanity attains finite nature,

---

[19] Stumpf, S.E. (1993) Elements of Philosophy; An Introduction (3rd Edition) McGraw-Hill Book Company/p33

The Positive Tiv Woman

Thomas Sankara once said, a bad son may be born but a bad mother does not exist. A good woman is Shima I orya i.e. the heart of the householder. She is an embodiment of wisdom of knowledge and is far more precious than jewels. The heart of her husband trusts in her. She affects the life of her husband so much that life without her has no meaning. *Demelu Koko* (199)_yery ably chronicles the Tiv experience in this regard,

> A *woman who wants to affect her husband's life would herself ask for an assistant, thus allowing her husband to marry a junior wife. Sometimes the senior wife would make the choice herself which in itself was an act of courtesy to a respected husband. This enabled the senior wife to stay the compound and fix the favorite food of her husband and receive the respect due to her as a senior wife; Mother.*[20]

The words of the book or proverbs chapter 31 fit very well with the Tiv understanding of the positive woman. In part, it states that, "her children rise up and call her blessed; her husband praises her, many women have done excellently, but you surpass them all" such is the desire of many women that Mrs. Ronald Reagan (1978:59) summed up in an interview. "I believe a woman's real happiness and fulfillment comes from within her home, with a husband and children". Another woman of substance Mrs. Golda Meir, (1978:58) the former Israeli Premier , was the outstanding career woman of our time, she achieved more in a man's world than any other woman in any century-and she did it on sheer ability, not on her looks, or her legs. She was repeatedly identified as the most admired woman in the world, yet she said without hesitation that "marriage and having babies is the most fulfilling thing a woman can ever do"[21].

Similarly, Madam Mbakaan Tsezughul a positive Tiv woman had a very successful business career to the envy of all in Tivland, though, conceded that her crushing disappointment was that she never has a child of her own in the house of a caring and protective husband. Another positive Tiv woman, Madam Abunde Zer who herself lived an unfulfilled life without a caring and loving husband was constrained to regenerate her extinct family having failed to have children of her own. These examples represent the share of sorrows and sufferings of unfulfilled desires and bitter defeats of the positive Tiv women. They are never ever crushed by life's disappointments.

---

[20] Koko, D.W. (1999) Recorded interview at Tse-Agberagba, Konshisha L.G.C. on 20th Sept.
[21] Meir G (1978) in Schlafly, The Power of the Positive Woman New York, Jove Publications Inc.p58

Their positive. TheHk-afe mental attitude has equipped them with an inner security that the actions of men and society can never fracture. Their problems, and travails are not a conspiracy against them in a "man's world", but a challenge to their capabilities. Such challenges are not construed as act targeted at discriminating against them, neither are they covert or overt disadvantages in life nor acts of enslavement from which thet' energies will be called to action to liberate hefsetf

Tiv women are not slaves and so do not beckon on anybody for emancipation and equality with the men. Tiv women in their chorused opinion are beneficiaries of an egalitarian society. They are not lured by what seem to women outside Tiv society as the glory of the male regime. The way to a glorious top, they say, is not, and cannot come by mere symbolic imitation of the male or doing better what a man can do. Mrs. Monica Ushir (2000) analogously argues out the point thus: "woman has her own peculiar glory as different from man's glory as is the glory of the moon from that of the sun, as is that of the shine of silver from the shine of gold". Men and women, she says, play complimentary roles arising from the basic difference in their creative energies, which reflects a fundamental division in nature itself into polar opposites of positive and negative forces and potentials, which compliment and supplement each other in running the world.

Unarguably, man's creative energies are centrifugal, outgoing. He goes forth to conquer the world. On the other hand, Woman's creative energies are centripetal, inwardturned and concerned with conserving, sustaining and developing what has been received. To the extent that man and woman compliment and supplement each other, the issue of liberation becomes nonsensical verbiage, for all of man's accomplishments are central to her being. It follows from this conclusion that, in traditional Tiv society, woman is a centered being of beings. All that man and society need is vested in the woman. She carries in her the children the husband and the society. As one woman says, men are like the headlines of a newspaper, and women are the details[22] The man as male cannot be indefinitely centrifugal in expanding energy unless there is a center on which he can draw and to which he can return for recuperation, and the woman as female can and do provide the natural resources effective check to avoid disastrous and fragmented Tiv society. *The Story of Adan -Wade*[23] the first classical novel from the Tiv and about the Tiv is a typical

22   The guardian 20.8.2005:p29),
23   Chia, S. (2001) Adan-Wade Kohol Ga (The story of Ada||-Wade; A Tiv classic),Translated with Introduction by Akosu, T; Makurdi Abogun Printing and paper wills Ltd p

example in this regard. It is thus the mind set of the Tiv woman to conclude in the words of I.K Zanny (1999:869) that:

> *The greatest glory of a woman is... to provide vehicles for the egos that are to come into incarnation, and to preside over a home in which her children can be properly and happily trained to live (heir life and to do their work in the world ... it is the greatest glory of the feminine incarnation, the great opportunity which women have and men have not. Men have other opportunities, but that really wonderful privilege of motherhood is not theirs. It is the women who do this great work for helping the world, for the continuance of the race[24],*

Speaking with the mindset of a Tiv woman, Clara Codd herself a woman, appeals to the woman of the world whom she believed needs not liberation and centering as empowerment thus:

> *The real work of women in the building of the new era and the salvation of the future humanity is only just beginning. we must help to bring back to the world the eternally true ideal and conception of woman, her place and work in nature. We must cease to copy men, and dare to be ourselves; discover and organize the real education, the real work, the real function, in nature which belongs to woman, those which will develop her peculiar faculties and make her strong beautiful, pure, intuitive a miniature mother of God, and Mater consolatrix to the world[25]*

It thus proves our point that the Tiv woman is not an instrument of exploitation, the quality of her powers and those of the men are simply distinct one from the other. The woman's powers are silent, while the man's power are power of thunder. A combination of the two is what comes down as a state of enlightenment and refinement as opposed to a state of barbarism, which is a reigning virtue now. The suggestion here in that, Tiv society is founded on the solidarity of the family, base on man and woman enacting well their natural complimentary roles so as to avoid the disintegration of *Tar Tiv*. What the Tiv woman needs in this age of violence and ugliness in the land is further empowerment, to act out her complimentary role of conserving, sustaining, silent background to transform and accomplish the man's outer, centrifugal energies. Such is when the Tivw ould say, *Wan **Ushir** Kwase wam, uma yo ka cii jene.* i.e the revered daughter of Ushir my dear wife, such is the being of man. The Tiv do not argue like Aristotle that "the female is a female

---

24 Zatmey, **LK.** (1999) **"Women's Liberation for the** New Nascent **civilization" inthe**   Theosophist vo p869
[25] Ibid pp869-870

by virtue of a certain lack of qualities afflicted with a natural defectiveness" or like St. Thomas Aquinas, who pronounced woman to be an "imperfect man," an "incidental" being symbolized in Genesis where Eve is depicted as made from what Bossuet called "a supernumerary bone" of Adam[26]. For the Tiv and among the Tiv, man as male has no essential meaning in itself quite apart from the woman as female. Indeed, the Tiv man cannot think of himself without woman and so he eulogizes womanhood as *pende-tyo* (head rest), the brain box, a centre on which he draws beingness, energy and to which he returns for true essential human nature.

Thus argued, it is a grievous error for the Tiv woman to hide herself in shame and act out roles that tend to imitate man symbolically believing same to be glorious, I.K Zanney (1999:869) speaks eloquently against this thinking that, "one great mistake women are making in their struggle for emancipating and equality with men is that, wrongly allured by what they see as the glory of the male regime, they think that the way for a woman to be glorious is to imitate man symbolically, say to wear trouser instead of the skirt... Woman has her own peculiar glory as different from man's glory..."[27] Truly understood though, empowerment is not rubbing shoulders with men, but feeling good about oneself and having confidence to walk into the future genuinely and truly as a woman acting out her being as such.

The positive Tiv woman; the good and beautiful woman combines intrinsic and extrinsic qualities of manners (inja) and good look (rmpoom) respectively to qualify as *Shima-I-Orya*, intrinsic qualities of honesty, chastity, humility, compassion, commitment, care, respect and altruism (emphasis mine) are complimented with her extrinsic qualities of good looks and hardwork. She stands out as a shinning example in her community and always referred to by other men in the community as a living example of an ideal wife. Her beauty is not only of the body but also of the mind,

---

[26] Stumpf op. cit p155
[27] I.K. Zenny, ibid p869

Conclusion

"... Lord give me the strength to change what I can change, the serenity to accept what I cannot change and the wisdom to discern the difference ".

The above quip is the happy assertion of the Tiv women in acknowledgement of the leading role of man as the head of the home. No doubt, significant change has taken place in Tiv land. This change obviously affects the traditional roles and status of women. However the esteemed, respected and honoured position of the Tiv woman in economy, agriculture, politics and home affairs still subsists, Tiv men are householders though, that never mean their women are voiceless beast controlled by male lords. There is nothing on earth that the Tiv esteems so highly as their women, the most liberated in Nigeria, in fact,

agitated feminism common among today's woman is near absent in Tiv society. The Tiv are not quite aware of suppression or oppression. Perhaps, what a few of them describe as marginalization, oppression or discrimination is better understood as the general experience of all Nigerians in the distressed nation. Yet, Tiv are better placed than their Northern and Southern counterparts[28]. Though reported to be suffering from patriarchal oppression, the Tiv women themselves say they are satisfied with their position. (Oluwole and Ihuah 2003). The mere absence of malevolent sexism in Tiv society has promoted a vibrant tradition of Tiv women who held positions of importance and relevance in economic and political spheres in Tiv land.

Thus argued, the acquisition of foreign civilization (including Christianity and Islam) and its use as a value trade-off by African women is most dangerous. They have got a mess of porridge but they have lost their birth right. Bernadette Kunanmbi, (1978:151) eloquently states the dilemma of the African woman thus, "while Christianity and western type of education gave the African woman the feeling of independence and the ability to stand on her own to make decisions both in family and in society, it robbed her of the traditional protection of the extended family system and

---

28 Read Awe, Awe, B (1979) "The Yoruba Women in Traditional Society" in GanganIbadan, issue No, ; Imam, A (1998) The Household: Where are we now? In a Seminar on Changing Household Kingship and Gender Relations in Africa. CODESRIAAJNESOCO/AAWPRD Dakar, Senegal; Mba, N. (1987) Nigerian Women Mobilized; Political Activity in Southern Nigeria, 1990-1996, Berkeley, Institute of International Studies, University of California; Okonjo, K (1987) "The Dual-sex political systems of operation; Igbo women and community politics in Mid-Western Nigeria" in Nancy J. Hafkin and Edna G. Bay, (ds) Women in Africa; *Studies in Social and Economic Change.* Standford, California, Standford University Press; Oluwole, S.B, and Ihuah S.A.(2003) *Gender and Constitutionalism:* (Final Report prepared by Centre for African Culture and Development: CEFACAD, for Centre for Constitution and Governance; CCG).

of the society, which in the past was the cornerstone of stability in family life... She is gaining what she wants, but losing what she needs".[29] For humanity to realize its full potential therefore, there is urgent need for women to realize their true nature and the profound spiritual power for good which resides in that nature; they must take their due complimentary place beside men and assume their true, essential role. Then a saner order and a better civilization may come into being. The Tiv woman like every other woman in Africa surely need further empowerment, however, the struggle for its attainment needs to go beyond liberation and beyond centering towards genuine sharing of functional roles between the two halves of Africa, male and female, Simone de Beauwoir Sums up this thinking ambivalently that, "man seeks in woman the other as Nature and as his fellow being... He exploits her, but she crushes him, he is born of her and dies in her, she is the source of his being and the reason that he subjugates to his will; Nature is a vein of gross material in which the soul is imprisoned, and she is the supreme reality... Woman sums up nature as Mother, Wife, and Idea.,."[30] That women stand opposed to the men is a primordial reality. But they do not in themselves as a group constitutes a separate group similar to the proletariat or bourgeoisie which as a class can think of themselves as separate from the other class. In human interaction, the question is after all, not what women and men are, or whether there are innate psychological differences between the sexes, but what kind of society is morally justifiable. To this question, society must appeal to the notions of justice, equity and liberty. Male and female is a fundamental unity with its two halves riveted together, and the cleavage of society along the line of sex is nothing but retrograde.

Woman is a female, and man is a male, different as biological facts though, they both seek in each, the other and the being of their beings. There is, as one would say, a whole world of significance which exists only through their communicative behaviour, this alone is the substance of their acts and sentiments, the incarnation of all the values that call out their free activity.

---

[29] Bernadette Kunanmbi, (1978:151)
[30] Beauvoir, S. (1993) The Second Sex in Stumpf, S.E, Elements of Philosophy: An Introduction New York,McGrow Hill, Inc.159-160

REFERENCES

Aahire,P.T.(ed) (1993) The Tiv in Nigeria, Zaria Tiv studies project

Abuul, G. (2000) Recorded interview in Makurdi on *fatf** May.

Amao - Kehinde, A,O. (2000) A Course text on human Development and Learning, Lagos.

Amina, M, (1995) "Democracy or Femocracy? State feminism and Democratization in Nigeria", in African Development.

Angya, C (2002) Lecturer house wife recorded interview in Makurdi on 20 August, at Makurdi.

Anshi, M.W. (2004) IEREN: An Introduction to Tiv Philosophy, Makurdi, Obeta Continental Press.

Ardener, S, (U.1975) Perceiving women, London Mulby Press.

Awe, B (1979) "The Yoruba Women in Traditional Society" in Gangan Ibadan, issue No,

Ayua, N. (2002) Praise Singer Cited Courtesy of Gwaza uja-Matyo, Broadcaster in Makurdi, recorded interview on 20th May.

Beattie, J and Middleton, J. (1969) "Spirit possession and Mediumship" in Africa, Oxford, Oxford University Press.,

Beauvoir, S. (1993) The Second Sex in Stumpf, S.E, Elements of Philosophy: An Introduction New York, McGrow-Hill, Inc.

Chia, S. (2001) Adalft-Wade Kohol Ga (The story of Ada||-Wade; A Tiv classic) Translated with Introduction by Akosu, T; Makurdi Abogun Printing and paper wills Ltd.

Imam, A (1998) The Household: Where are we now? In a Seminar on Changing Household Kingship and Gender Relations in Africa. CODESRIAAJNESOCO/AAWPRD Dakar, Senegal.

Ityavyar, D. (1992) The Changing socio-political role of Tiv women, Jos, University of Jos Press.

Janambi, B. (1978) "The place of women in Christianity," in Shorter Aylward, African Christian Theology, New York, Oirbis Books.

Koko, D.W. (1999) Recorded interview at Tse-Agberagba, Konshisha L.G.C. on 20th Sept.

KopytorT, I. (1971) "Ancestors as Elders," in Africa Vol. 41 No. 2.

Kureve, B. I. (2002) Recorded in Interview on the 16th January 2001 at Makurdi. Laudes R. (1953) "Negro slavery and Female Status," in African Affairs Vol. 15 No. 2.

Kwase Tiv stands for, **The Positive Tiv** Woman.

Mazrui, A.A. (1991) "The Black Woman and the Problem of Gender. Trials Triumphs and Challenges" Being the 1991 Guardian Lecture Delivered on July 4, 1991.

Mba, N. (1987) Nigerian Women Mobilized; Political Activity in Southern Nigeria, 1990-1996, Berkeley, Institute of International Studies, University of California.

Meir G (1978) in Schlafly, The Power of the Positive Woman New York, Jove Publications Inc.

Momoh, C.S.(1978) "Eldership in African Marriages" in African Insight, Vol. 18 No. 1. Spring.

Obbo, C, (1980) African Women; Their Struggle for Economic Independence, London, Hutzhinson & Co (publihsers) Ltd.,

Okonjo, K (1987) "The Dual-sex political systems of operation; Igbo women and community politics in Mid-Western Nigeria" in Nancy J. Hafkin and Edna G. Bay, (ds) Women in Africa; *Studies in Social and Economic Change*. Standford, California, Standford University Press.

Oluwole, S.B, and Ihuah S.A.(2003) *Gender and Constitutionalism:* (Final Report prepared by Centre for African Culture and Development: CEFACAD, for Centre for Constitution and Governance; CCG).

Oluwole, S.B. (1997) "Culture , gender and Development Theories in Africa", in Africa Development, Dakar, CODESR1A.

Pritchard, E.E. (1965) *The Position of Women in Primitive Societies and. Other Essays,* Oxford University Press.

Reagan, R. (1978) in Schlafly, The Power of the Positive Woman.

Rubingh, E. (1969) Sons of Tiv, Grande Rapids, Michigan, Baker Book House Company.

Sani, H. (2001) *Women and National Development: The Way Forward,* Ibadan, Spectrum Books Ltd.

Stumpf, S.E. (1993) Elements of Philosophy; An Introduction (3rd Edition) McGraw-Hill Book Company/

UShir, M,A, (2000) Hosue^f Wife/Teaeheri recorded Interview   on 10   December at Naka, Gwer-West Local Government Area, Benue State.

Yuhe, D,V, (1978) The Encounter of Tiv Religious and Moral Values with Catholicism in the Time of Secularism, Rome, Pont, Universtitatem S. Thomae.

Zatmey, **L .K.** (1999) **"Women's Liberation for the** New Nascent **civilization" in the** Theosophist vol. 120 No, 10pp. **868-870.**